BY JENNIFER FIERRO
AND GENEVIEVE FIERRO

Dedications

To my left arm, my Genevieve.

To my right arm, my Mommy.

Cuddle up,
nice and cozy,
and let me
tell you
a story.

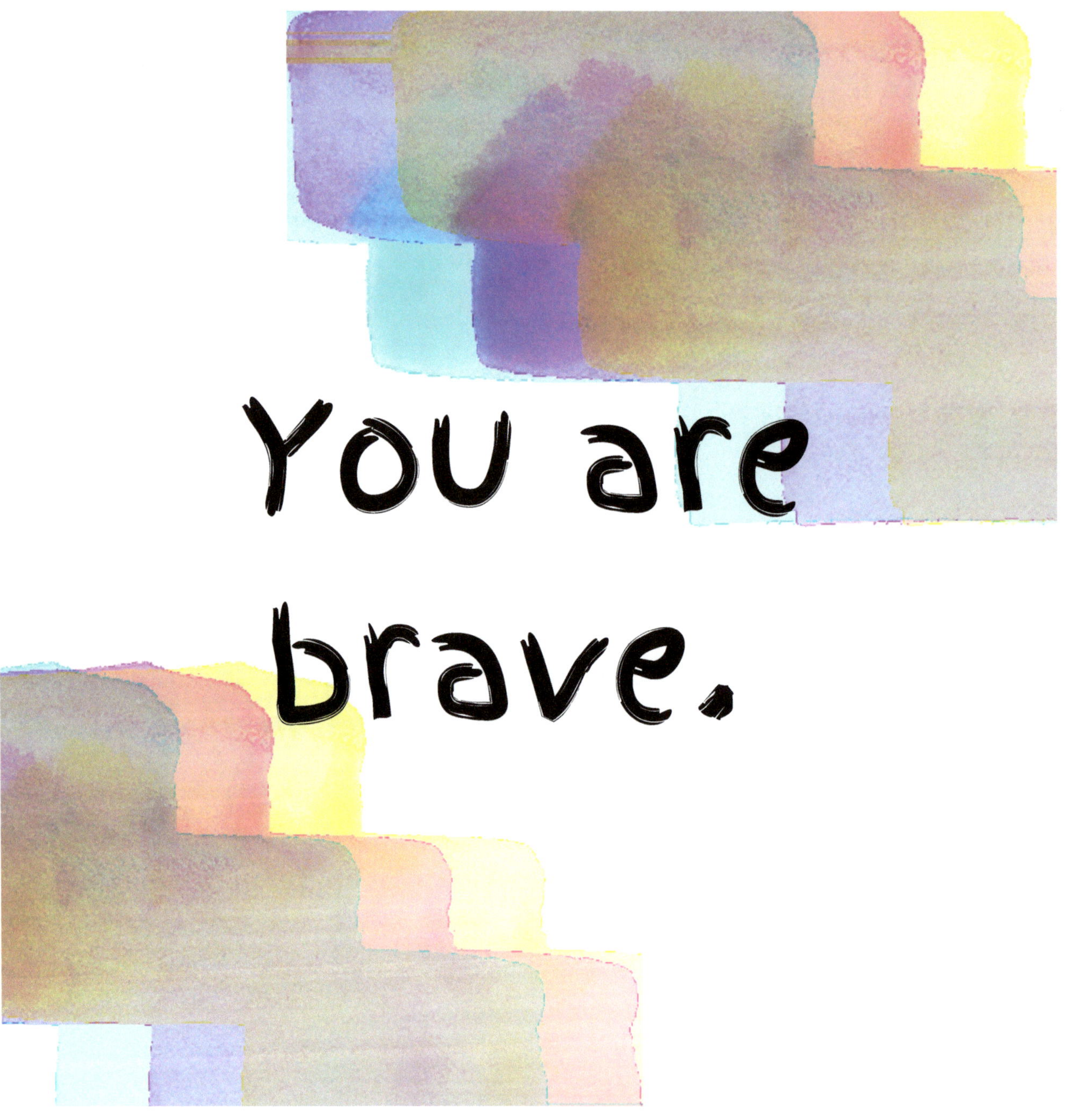

You are
brave.

You are
strong.

You are amazing in every way.

You are here and you matter to me.

You are
everything
good
in this world.

Now, let me tell you
the story of how much
I love you.

I love you
more than all
of the drops in the ocean.

I love you
more than all
of the stars in the sky.

I love you
more
than
the
warmth
of
the sun.

I love you
more
than
every
blade
of grass.

I love you
more than
every wish
ever made
on a
wishing
flower.

I love you
more than
every grain
of sand.

I love you
more
than
all of
the
books
ever
read.

I love you more than playing with bubbles.

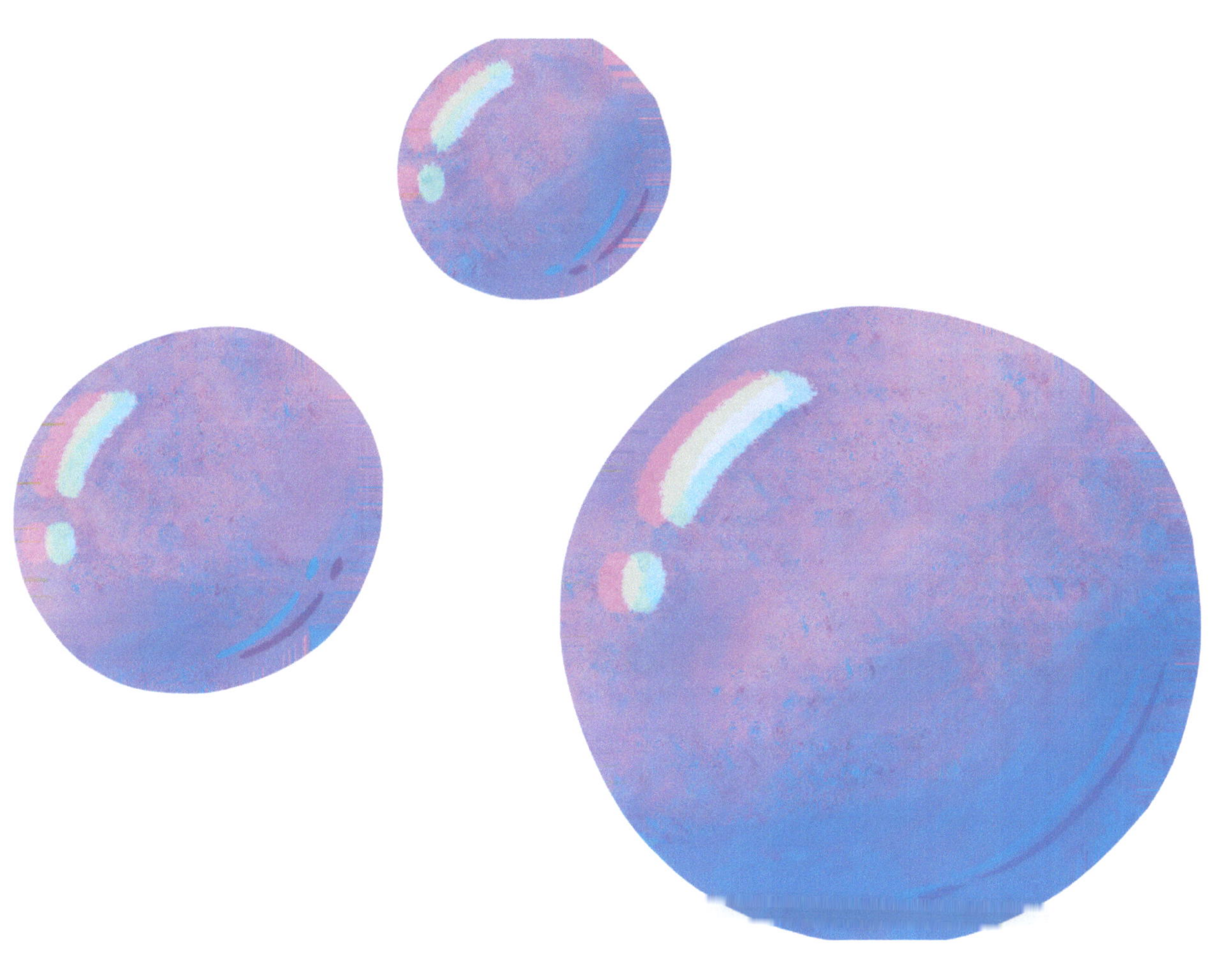

I
love you
more
than
balloons
at a
county fair.

I love you more
than all of the trees
ever planted.

I love you
more than
all of the
paintings
ever made.

I
love
you
more
than
fireworks.

I love you
more than
surprise
dance
parties.

I love you
more than
the highs
and lows.

My love for you has no limits.

My love for you
has   no
ending.

I see you, I love you,

I love you here. I love you now. I love you, always.

About
the Authors

Jennifer and Genevieve are a mother and daughter team in everything they do. Both enjoy reading, playing dolls together, and the color pink.